Discovering
HORSE BRASSES

John Vince

Shire Publication Ltd.

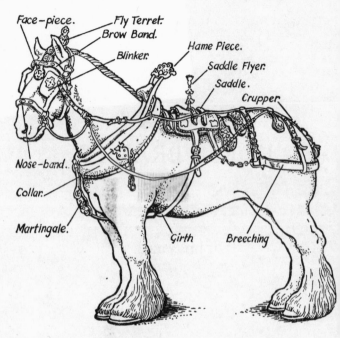

Shire horse and its harness

Copyright©1968 by John Vince. No. 44 in the 'Discovering' series. First published 1968; reprinted 1970, 1972, 1974, 1977, 1979, 1981. ISBN 0 85263 014 X.

Printed in Great Britain by C. I. Thomas & Sons (Haverfordwest) Ltd, Press Buildings, Merlins Bridge, Haverfordwest.

CONTENTS

ACKNOWLEDGEMENTS

The Author wishes to acknowledge the co-operation of the Hull Museum which allowed its collection of horse brasses to be photographed. These outstanding specimens may be seen at the Transport Museum, High Street, Hull.

BIBLIOGRAPHY

Brown, R. A.: *HORSE BRASSES—Their History and Origin;* 3rd Edition 1963. Available from—R. A. Brown, 65 Medfield Road, Roehampton, S.W.15. The author is secretary of the Hackney Horse Society. Illustrations line and half tone.

Evans, George Ewart: *THE HORSE IN THE FURROW;* 1960; Faber and Faber. An outstanding book with all the qualities of a standard work. Contains a chapter on horse brasses. Illustrated with C. F. Tunnicliffe's splendid drawings.

Hartfield, George: *HORSE BRASSES;* 1965; Abelard-Schuman. A general history of horse brasses and their design.

Hughes, G. Bernard: *HORSE BRASSES;* 1956; Country Life. Only a quarter of this book is concerned with horse brasses but most collectors will wish to add it to their bookshelves. Informative text.

Richards, H. S.: *ALL ABOUT HORSE BRASSES;* Drew & Hopwood, Birmingham 3. Published in 1943. Contains many illustrations showing the considerable variety of designs to be encountered.

SOCIETY

National Horse Brass Society: Membership Secretary, G. T. Thompson, 20 Greenhill Road, Sandford, near Bristol.

ORIGINS

Lost in the twilight of history are the days when man began to give up hunting and secure part of his living from the land. The first farmers created the first civilizations. Man's efforts alone were not sufficient to till the soil. However advanced his civilization became he could not throw off the ever present elements. They surrounded him and they alone determined whether or not the harvest was a fruitful one. The forces of good and evil were wrapped in mystery. At a very early time in man's development he became aware of the power of the sun and of the moon. In a hostile world it was essential to be able to appease the forces of good and bad.

A feature in all primitive societies even today is the acceptance of the idea of the evil eye. This is something which is common throughout the world. It goes back to the roots of all civilization and to this notion we owe the many and varied charms which man has devised in order to avert catastrophe. The horse, and also in earlier days the ox, which pulled the plough was for thousands of years a very important source of power and needed all possible protection.

Far away beyond the distant Caspian Sea in Turkmenskaya archaeologists have unearthed amulets left behind by some of the world's earliest farmers in the fifth millennium B.C. Among these we find simple discs marked unmistakably with sunlike rays. There are no written records to tell us how these early agriculturists used their amulets. It is a fair guess that they would have been very much aware of the sun's power and could have used such charms to protect their livestock.

Much nearer home, from the cairn at Dyffryn Ardudwy (Merionethshire), polished stone pendants have been discovered which doubtless served as amulets. We cannot be sure that people used these as charms to protect their livestock but the strong probability remains. Even in this century farmers in Cumberland used stones with natural holes formed in them which they hung around cows' necks or on the byre door.

One of the most interesting English finds dates from Roman times. The bronze bull's head found at Wilcote (Oxon.) clearly shows us that the animal had a roundel on its forehead. In Roman days the oxen pulled the plough and we can be reasonably certain that the use of this type of amulet dates at least from this period.

The Celtic era which followed provides us with what may be one of the earliest existing 'brasses'. This was illustrated in the catalogue of the National Museum of Scotland (1892) and shows a leaf shaped silver plate bearing a sun wheel at its apex. A number of other delicate and probably significant patterns also appear. These include two whorl patterns formed into triskele designs. We often see these represented as three conjoined legs—an emblem used by Manxmen. Its origin lies within the sun wheel design and it appears in Scandinavian decoration of the earlier Bronze Age, and upon the shields of Greek warriors. We can see therefore just how widespread its use really was. The fact that a horse's head is also shown on this particular plate also helps to persuade us that it was a horse charm. This silver specimen would have belonged to a chieftain or noble-man. It was found at Norries Law, Fifeshire.

Another find from the Celtic period (the Tal-y-Llyn Hoard —described in *Antiquity* XXXVIII, 149 (1964)) shows that even warriors used the triskele on their shields. We can appreciate how the emblem became used as a charm to protect man's domestic animals.

One of the difficulties in tracing the usage of amulets is the lack of any supporting documentary evidence. They came into being long before written history began and as they were objects tinged with superstition they never received any attention from the clerical historians of the Dark Ages. Until early mediaeval times there is nothing to be gleaned from written records. Illuminated manuscripts do give us a few slender clues about the types of implements used in distant days ; but such things were no more than small embellish-ments to a page border and very little detail has survived. The quality of the draughtsmanship in those times was very uneven and to the smallness of the pictures we can add the limitations imposed by the artists' skill.

The age of chivalry adds a little to our knowledge. The rich caparisons of the horses used in the joust and on the battlefield show that in addition to various forms of armour the war horse was decorated with plumes that had no func-tional purpose at all. In the list of horse breeds on page 8 the connection between the Old English War Horse and the Shire Horse is mentioned. The plumes on the horse drawing the brewer's dray seem to be a survival from jousting days, and the relationship becomes stronger when we remember the Shire's ancestors.

It should not be forgotten that folklore provides a strong bond with the remote past and we cannot underrate its importance when considering the form the horse brass took up to the last century. Eighteenth century brasses do not seem to have survived and perhaps they all found their way into the melting pot in Victoria's reign. The power of very old ideas is still discernible in the countryside and a century ago it was even stronger. In Norfolk, back in 1859, an instance is recorded of a ploughman who always had tied around the neck of his horse the thumb of an old leather glove. When this was stolen by mischievous boys it was found to contain a transcript of the Lord's Prayer. The ploughman claimed that this was an effective charm against the evil eye —one which preserved the horse from all manner of ills including stumbling. This kind of charm is on a parallel with the practice of the Pharisees. In Biblical times they placed a text of scripture in a small box on their foreheads, and it was a common custom for Jewish people to place a text on the lintel of their door. The natural stones used in Cumberland were mentioned above. They were also called witch's stones, and one belief was that the hole had been formed by the touch of an adder's tongue. The sprig of rowan tied to a cow's horn or hung in the cowshed is another ancient survival and harks back to the widely held beliefs about witchcraft.

No one has proved the continuity of the use of an amulet on horses or cattle ; so little documentary evidence is to be found. If old traditions did not endure how can we explain so many of the ancient symbols on the horse brasses described below. It is difficult to accept that the Victorian brass designers revived them of their own volition from a past that had not been recorded.

When we study horse brasses we are perhaps at first delighted or amazed at the tremendous variety of the designs and the whole subject seems to be rather bewildering. It is the object of this booklet to explain their main characteristics and to show why the really old ones are important in terms of the way in which they were made and for the folklore they represent.

HORSE POWER

To understand why such great numbers of brasses and so many designs remain from the last century one must realise the importance of the horse in the nineteenth century economy. First of all, there were several main breeds.

The Shire is a large and massive horse that was once the principal work horse in rural England. Apart from supplying the power for the farm plough the Shires also became dominant, in modern times, in London and other large towns as dray horses. The Shire horse is said to be the lineal descendant of the Old English War Horse found in so many mediaeval manuscripts. Its head is long and it is broad between the eyes. An arched neck, oblique shoulders and deep girth speak of its immense power. The feet are large and the heels wide. This breed was often crossed with the Clydesdale. Shires are usually black, brown or bay in colour and at 17 hands they are the heaviest horses in England. In the distant past they came from the Fenland. At the end of the last century Cambridge, Huntingdon, Lincoln, Nottingham, Leicester, Derby, Northampton, Warwick and Stafford were the main breeding counties.

The Suffolk Punch is a native breed from Norfolk, Suffolk and Essex. Horses brought by the Normans may have been the ancestors of this fine breed. They can be as tall as 16 hands. Their colours vary from chestnut to dark sorrel. The legs of this breed are lighter than those of the Shire and the feet are correspondingly smaller. On the claylands they were docile and willing workers.

The Cleveland Bay takes its name from the valley along the River Tees. Many of the horses used in pack horse days and in the coaching era came from this strain. Although they are light horses they were used for tillage on sandy soils. Their prevailing colour is bay with dark legs. From the Cleveland line the Yorkshire Coach Horse was developed. Cleveland Bays were almost as tall as the Shires and stood a good 16 hands.

The Clydesdale is another breed which takes its name from a valley. In Scotland it was the principal farm horse in the last century and its origin goes back several hundred years to the time a Duke of Hamilton imported a number of black stallions from Holland. The main colours are brown, bay and black. Chestnut and roan were colours to be avoided if you were buying. Clydesdales were about as tall as the Clevelands, but their well developed limbs made them more powerful.

The Hackney or Norfolk Trotter is partly descended from Norman ancestors. This was essentially a riding and trotting animal and it was obviously suited to the hackney carriages (that borrowed its name) which once abounded in London and other large towns. In colour it often resembled the Suffolks and it stood about 14 hands.

8

The Farm Horse

The number of horses required for a farm depended upon the total acreage. Three horses would be a minimum requirement for a mixed farm of about 100 acres, and one ploughman would be sufficient to attend to the tillage. On farms with 150 to 200 acres about five horses would be needed. Larger establishments of up to 500 acres would employ from seven to ten horses and about five ploughmen. The large farm with some 800 acres would need as many as fifteen or eighteen horses and eight ploughmen. A plough team of two, three or four horses could be expected to work up to 60 acres each year and while this figure may seem low by modern standards we must remember that ploughing was heavy work and absorbed a great deal of time.

One of the factors which determined the amount of time required to plough an acre of ground was the width of the furrow made by the plough. Furrows could vary from 8 to 12 inches across, and although the difference may seem small it had a significant effect on the total distance a horse had to travel. The best length of furrow was about 250 yards. A furlong (a furrow long) is 220 yards and many people have now forgotten how this old subdivision of a mile got its name. After centuries of use it will soon be lost as a meaningful measurement when we adopt the metric system. The time taken to plough an acre varied between six and eight hours.

Ploughmen started work early—at about 6 a.m. in the old days. When the horses had been fed and watered the ploughman returned home for a quick breakfast at 6.45. By 7.15 the team would start off to the field and ploughing began as soon as possible. To save the ploughman time children went to the field with his dinner when they came home from school at noon. If the field was a long way from home scholars went late to school in the afternoon. Many children had bad attendance records in the last years of the nineteenth century—when the agricultural depression made life a harsh affair for the large families which were then so common. Absences for boys and girls frequently amounted to 12 weeks at a time. One record of an absence of 26 weeks exists for a girl of ten years who was at work "picking stones in the fields". When every penny counted even the fruits of a child's labours became a significant part of a family budget.

For the ploughman work in the fields lasted until 3.30 or so in the winter and then the homeward journey began. In the stable the horse's needs were met before the ploughman went home for tea. His brief respite over, he then returned to the stable to attend to the harness and make ready for yet another day on the stubbles. If he was lucky his working day finished at 5.30 p.m. A good many men walked several miles to work in the time of the depression when labour was abundant and their walking and working hours must have been well above twelve each day.

Even though times were hard the ploughman took a pride in his team. One of the highlights of his year was the ploughing match when his horses appeared resplendent in their harness with brass amulets all a-glitter in the sun.

ENGLAND ON FOUR LEGS

We live in the age of the motor car and during the few years of its existence it has exercised a profound impact upon the shape and course of our road system. It is now rather difficult for us to imagine what road conditions were like in the days before even the canals had begun to carve their way across the English landscape. In those days horses were almost as numerous as men. Transport depended upon rivers —which did not always flow in the direction men wished to follow—or the roads. Since the Romans left these shores in the fifth century men had cared little for the roads they left behind and by the reign of Elizabeth I the best of our roads were not much better than cart tracks. The passage of heavy vehicles was difficult if not impossible and even today lonely and narrow pack horse bridges still help to remind us of the manner in which most things were carried before the eighteenth century saw a revived interest in communications. A large part of the wealth of mediaeval England came from the wool trade. From the twelfth century onwards the character of the wool trade changed slowly and instead of exporting the raw wool, England's weavers made her an important producer of cloth. Before the industrial era wool could be moved on a train of pack horses. Once the population began to expand however and enclosures of common land uprooted so many families—particularly in the eighteenth century—England's roadways became busy and dangerous places. As towns began to expand and the old self-sufficient independence of settlements began to evaporate, new needs arose and these could only be met by improving road communications. Following the Civil War, and perhaps because of it, things began to change and by the reign of Queen Anne the pace had quickened. Roads were repaired at the expense of the parish—and wagons rolled from all parts of England down them towards London. The capital was the focus of political and economic life and this fact alone played an important part in shaping the turnpike road system which has left such a strong imprint upon our current road maps.

The carriage itself is a modern innovation to these shores although its invention is ascribed to Erichthonius of Athens in 1486 B.C. As far as Europe is concerned it seems to have been used in France from the sixteenth century onwards. Closed carriages began to be used by persons of quality in Elizabeth I's reign. They were then known as whirlicotes. The use of a carriage by men was then considered to be effeminate and in 1601 a bill was brought before Parliament to make the practice illegal. It was repealed in 1625. As far back as 1619 the Duke of Buckingham used a carriage, presumably illegally, drawn by six horses. His rival the Earl of Northumberland drove eight horses and this is perhaps where one-upmanship on our roads began. By 1650 carriages could be hired in Paris where they operated from the Hotel Fiacre. St. Fiacre is the patron saint of cab drivers and he also gave his name to a type of carriage. This connection no doubt originated from the fortuitous name of the hotel. In England the development of coaching provided the Crown with another opportunity to increase its income and in 1747 the coach tax was introduced.

Post horses were originally intended for the post boys but later legislation in Charles II's time allowed postmasters to provide horses for travellers. Posting houses abounded along England's highways and they can usually still be identified by the wide archways which lead into courtyards that once were lined with stables. These if they remain will now almost certainly be used as garages. The tempo of coaching days was a swift one and post horses were often changed as quickly as possible—sometimes in one or two minutes—to allow the coach to pursue its journey. For this reason it seems coach horses did not wear the amulets so highly prized by the ploughman.

Fast coaches from Bristol to London could make the journey "in one day" like the coach which left the White Hart at 4.0 a.m. every morning. Travellers with more time to spare could take "a coach in two days" on Tuesdays, Thursdays or Saturdays and depart at the more orthodox time of 7.0 a.m. "Flying wagons with a guard" left from Peter Wiltshire's, Peter Street, Bristol every day at noon. On Wednesdays and Saturdays from Fromont and Holbrook's warehouse at Broadmead other flying wagons set out for

Blossom's Inn, Cheapside. We do not know if the horses pulling these fast goods wagons displayed amulets but it seems certain that the teams would be changed several times on the way to London and we can guess that brasses were probably not worn. The horse brass tradition seems to have remained mainly in the country and with the local London carriers.

An indication of the horse population in England at the beginning of the nineteenth century is given by the *Posse Comitatus*, a census undertaken in 1798 when a Napoleonic invasion was feared. In Buckinghamshire the distribution in some towns was as follows:

	Men	Horses	Wagons	Carts
Buckingham	217	50	19	34
Beaconsfield	246	119	39	61
Ivinghoe	97	49	8	22
Drayton Parslow	96	59	8	28
Winslow	242	69	17	38
Great Marlow	632	229	73	88
Saunderton	51	50	12	16

The horse population of the whole country, therefore, must have run into millions and increased rapidly throughout the nineteenth century until the coming of the motor car curtailed it.

BRASS MANUFACTURE

Since man discovered metal in the rocks beneath his feet it has been a highly prized and polished material. Historians have suggested that the first metal man used was the copper which was once found in more or less a pure state in certain parts of the Middle East. The first smelting was probably a fortunate accident. From primitive stone implements man graduated to copper then bronze (a mixture of tin and copper) and finally iron. The qualities of iron made it the supreme material for both weapons and ploughshares. Even today, among primitive societies, those who know and exploit the secrets of ironworking enjoy a special social position.

In mediaeval Europe metalworkers used an alloy, known by the popular name of latten, which consisted of copper (60%), zinc (30%), lead and tin (10%). This type of material was produced in Roman times and its warm yellow colour made it a suitable substitute for gold. For decorative purposes it provided a hard-wearing surface which could retain its brilliance for long periods.

During the middle ages the metals were extracted and then blended together before they were cast into relatively small sheets. These in turn were hammered into some sort of uniform thickness before they were engraved to become the memorial brasses which we can still find in abundance in many of our parish and cathedral churches—see *Discovering Brasses* by Malcolm Cook, Shire Publications (25p).

Horse brasses made from such sheets of latten form some of the earliest surviving examples from a very long and ancient line of amulets. Horse brasses with hammered reverse sides could be as old as the eighteenth century but their number is indeed small nowadays. An astute collector will look at both sides with care to try to spot any vestigial hammer marks. These marks, in addition to the colour and thickness of the metal, may help him to decide upon the probable antiquity of the specimen. Hammered finishes do not always denote age and a box full of such brasses reclining among the bric-a-brac of a junk shop will not always represent a hoard of ancient origin. Such a "discovery" needs to be approached with some degree of reservation.

At about the beginning of Victoria's reign a significant change was introduced into the horse brass world. Up to that time the designs were probably fairly simple and could be adequately fashioned with a punch and file from a flat sheet. The introduction of cast brasses allowed the use of more complex emblems, and it is from the wealth of nineteenth century patterns that the illustrations in this book are drawn.

The surface colour of the metal could be modified in two principal ways. One of the easiest devices was to add a mellowness to the metal by a sequence of immersions in acid solution. Other brasses were coated with a lacquer. Some had a silvered finish—possibly to withstand the effects of a briny atmosphere in coastal areas.

Patterns for cast brasses were carved with considerable skill and precision in close grained pearwood. From this pattern the sand mould was prepared and into it the molten metal was poured. The finishing was then undertaken by hand and rough edges were removed with a file. Other features of the design were enhanced at this stage and the brass was provided with a final polish before it was dispatched to the harness maker. During the casting process short stubs were formed on the reverse side of the brass to allow it to be held in a vice. When the polishing had been completed these stubs were removed with a file, but some brasses will still show traces of them if they are inspected with care.

A number of different names were given to the various kinds of brass used in the eighteenth century. The invention of prince's metal was attributed to Prince Rupert — nephew of Charles I—but it seems more likely that he simply favoured its use or was perhaps responsible for its introduction into England. Pinchbeck and Muntz (of Birmingham) also gave their names to the alloys they prepared and to these we may add orichalc, mosaic gold and yellow metal.

HORSE BRASS DESIGN

(The numbers in brackets refer to the illustrations on the centre pages of this book.)

THE SUN

One of the earliest of man's symbols was the sun. We can find the sun displaying a rotund face (57) or faceless with radiant arms. Many other designs also reflect this idea (26, 56, 61, 96). Three of the brasses shown (59, 95, 97) have wide centres made up of concentric circles and this symbol is of immense antiquity. The round centre represents the earth and the rings surrounding it are the waters of the oceans which in turn are enclosed by the heavens.

An interesting variation of the sun brass is the one (60) with seven arms which radiate from the centre and terminate in trefoils. Seven has been a magic number for thousands of years and doubtless it was with this quality in mind that this particular brass was designed.

The sun brass with a face (57) is very similar to the Sun fire marks which can still be seen on hundreds of buildings throughout the country. These were issued by the Sun Fire Office which was founded in 1710. In the early days the various fire insurance companies maintained their own fire engines in the larger towns and this particular design may be based on a brass which could have been worn by a horse in a fire engine team. The sun of course is a fairly common charge in heraldry and among the many famous families which have made use of it are the Staffords, Dukes of Buckingham, who at various times used seventeen different badges in addition to the Stafford Arms. (A Coat of Arms belongs to a family but a badge, which may or may not reflect the Arms, was often used as a personal symbol by a member of a family for his own convenience.)

14

In Bronze Age Denmark the sun symbol took the form of a simple circle. This often had spokes among other additions, and so the emblem of the sun-wheel was evolved (63, 87, 14). Brasses bearing sun wheels are usually flat with a simple cut out pattern. Less frequently we find the kind (76) which is composed of two discs. The smaller one is arranged so that it can rotate, adding its own note to the rhythm of the harness. In addition to the curved rays of the sun wheel this brass also shows ten moons in the spaces between its spokes. Although eight is a useful number to employ when dividing a circular design odd numbers often occur among the sun brasses. We find on some the mystic number seven (60, 107) used to delineate the sun's rays, and nine (13) on others. Considerably more skill was required to fashion a design with an odd number of divisions; and the craftsman who made the matrix was clearly a master of his art.

The device (27) may have started out as a sun wheel, but it also has a heraldic name—a carbuncle. Carbuncles are used as a charge—an ornament on the plain background of the shield—and this kind of figure also helped to add strength to a shield if it was fashioned with iron bands. Among those who employed a carbuncle (or escarbuncle, to use an alternative form) was Henry II—who used it as a badge—and Queen Berengaria of Navarre, wife of Richard I, who displayed a golden carbuncle upon a red shield, and it may be that her device endured long enough to become a traditional emblem of the brass maker. There is another explanation for an emblem of this kind. Its eight spokes make a double cross, containing the Greek *chi* and a cross. A less probable alternative is that it represents a Coptic Cross with the four nails that join it at the centre. The many variations of the cross symbol are discussed more fully in another chapter.

THE MOON AND STARS

As the art of heraldry developed in the early middle ages many shields were emblazoned with the moon emblem, the crescent. In heraldry the usual form it takes is with its points uppermost and in this position it is called, heraldically, a simple crescent. It indicates in heraldry the second son in a family and when used in this way it is called a mark of cadence. On shields the crescent also appears in two other positions. If its horns point towards the left, that is the dexter side of the shield, it is said to be increscent; but in the opposite position, pointing towards the sinister side, it is said to be decrescent. An upside down crescent is extremely rare in English heraldry although in other parts of the world this is its common position. In the Arms of the City of Portsmouth we may find the crescent and the star together and these emblems combined have also been attributed to King Richard I and King John. It seems highly probable that the crescent was introduced into English heraldry partly by the Crusaders who returned home with trophies of war which were embellished with both the crescent and the star.

One can find a tremendous variety of crescents among English horse brasses and those shown in the plates give some indication of the typical designs the collector may expect to encounter. In 68, 71, 72, 73, 89, 90, 91 most of the crescents point upwards. One (70) suggests a crescent within a crescent and as a result has four points. Crescents enclosing stars also appear (73, 77, 90, 105, 108) and these examples give some idea of the ingenuity of the brass maker. The interesting specimen (93) with points facing downwards has three six-pointed stars punched into it. Two of the brasses (7, 8) seem to contain a sun-wheel instead of a simple star. The collector will meet many other variations on this theme, all of them are equally fascinating. There is one very unusual crescent to be found (72) and this encloses a heart, a symbol of the inner life. The antiquity of this latter symbol can scarcely be measured and it is not surprising to find it (17, 18, 19) occurring so often on the horse brass. Unusual combinations of crescents may sometimes be found. One (92) shows three crescents joined at their bases to form an attractive and perhaps highly significant symbol.

Although the crescent is a symbol of moon worship its appearance on the English horse brass stems probably from the heraldic charge used by local lords. The use of heraldic devices would have been a useful arrangement in times when most people could not read and relied on pictorial signs. To use brasses which served the dual purpose by protecting the horse and also displaying the manorial lord's device would have been politic, a show of deference to one's landlord. A symbol from the lord's arms chinking on the plough horse's harness could suggest that the ploughman accepted his feudal relationship with the manorial lord. At least it provided an outward sign that this was so.

THE SIGN OF THE CROSS

The central emblem of the Christian Faith is the sign of the cross and from the start of the Christian era the

Courtesy of Steward & Patteson Ltd., a member of the Watney Mann Group.

John and Bill — two percheron horses — with a van. On the martingales the brasses include a windmill and a talbot. Plumes adorn their plaited manes.

Odds and ends

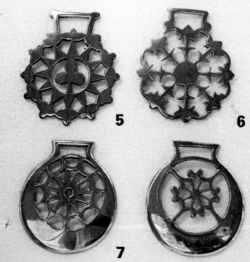

1, 2, 4:
Geometrical
designs. 3:
moline quad
heraldic.

5. Playing c
brass: Ace
with twelve
to represent
rest of the
6: An eight
cross. 7, 8:
wheels in a
crescent —
has eleven r

9, 10, 11: Horseshoe
brasses with eight
spokes. 10, 11: Sun
wheel. 12, 15: Sun
wheels in a
crescent —
variations of 7 &
8.

13: Sun wheel
design with nine
spokes — note the
odd number.
14. An ancient
form of sun wheel
often found in
Danish art.
16: Geometrical.

17: Heart brass with floral boss. 18: Heart design in openwork border. 19: conjoined hearts — ea heart meets two others form a prim number.

20: Crest — lion passant 21: Crest — a stag tripp 22: A lion ra 23: Crest — talbot passa

24: Star. 25:
Cross potent
within a
classical
border.
: Sun wheel
and rays.
Escarbuncle
— heraldic.

28: Bell brass
with three
chimes.
9: Bell within
a crescent-
tice how the
coating has
been worn
way from the
upper edge.
30: A single
chime with
even pierced
holes. 31:
Twin chime.

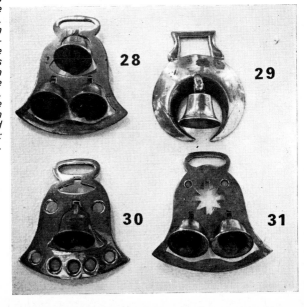

32: Acorns in a cluster.
33: Wheats in a cresce..
34: Stampe.. wheatsheaf design on .. plate — a rather crude.. pattern. 35:.. Acorn — e..

36, 37: Geometrical.. shields.
38: Wheats.. in a cresce..
39: Wheats.. in a delicate.. border.

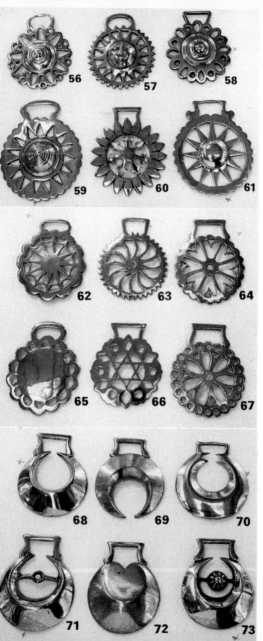

56-63, 65: Sundiscs. 60: Sundisc with seven rays — a lucky number.

64: Heraldic Maltese cross. 66: Star of David. 67: A double cross.

68-73: Crescents. 70: A crescent within a crescent. 72: A crescent containing a heart. 73: Star and crescent. 71 has its star missing.

74, 78: Geometrical.
75: Cross.
76: Sundisc with revolving sun wheel.
77, 79: Star and crescent.

80: Cross with thirteen holes in each quarter.
81: Crescent.
2, 85: Geometrical.
83: Fleur de lis — heraldic
84: Clover leaf made from a thin pressed sheet.

86: Geometrical containing a cross quadrate.
87: Sun wheel.
88: Geometrical.
89-91: Star and crescent.

92-94: Crescents.
95-97: Sundiscs with concentric bosses.

98, 101: Anchors
99: Scallop shell: a pilgrim sign. Made from a pressing like 84.
100: Sundisc with scalloped edges. 102: Shield with boss.
103: Bell brass without a bell.

104: Fleur de lis — heraldic. 105, 106, 108: Star and crescent.
107: Seven rayed sun wheel.
109: Geometrical.

110: Star of
d. 111-113,
and 115
emorative
brasses.
fford knot.

ortrait brass
good detail
ter brasses
om possess.
117-120:
memorative
brasses.
21: Star and
cent design.

23: Barrels.
127: Sacks.
125: Bell.
126: Ship.

128, 130: Horseshoe with a head. 129: Horse with harness. 131-133: Horse passant.

134: Unicorn in crescent. 135, Horse passant a horse shoe. 136, 138, 139, 142: Horse rampant. 137: Jockey.

140: Horse in harness 141: Horse passant in a border of horseshoes and legs. 143: Horseshoes. 145: Fanciful modern design— notice the impractical shape of the loop.

146, 147: Horse with harness. 148: Horse sant. 149: A broken brass. 50, 156: Same as 149 but intact and of a different size.

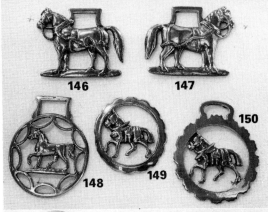

151: Crest — a horse's head. 152: Unicorn in a crescent. 153-155, 160: Horse rampant.

57: Non-heraldic horse. 158, 159, 161: Horse passant. 62: Racing horse.

163: Lion's head
164: Cat.
165: Griffin.
166: Camel.
167, 168: Lion rampant.

169: Stag couchant.
170: Pelican in her piety.
171: Raven.
172: Stag statant.
173: Cockerel.
174: Bear.

175-180: Horse figures.

Terrets:
199: Flower.
200: Shield.
201, 204:
Geometrical.
Probably not [...]
original centre[...]
— note the s[...]
202: Sundisc.
203: Crown a[...]
thistle.

205: Star.
206: Heart.
207: Wheel.
208: Thistle.
209: Acorn.
210: Crescent

cross has taken many different forms. It has been combined with other symbols; it has stood alone and the artist has embellished it. Wherever it has appeared its meaning has been equally well understood. It is no surprise to find among the rich symbolism of the horse brass many variations of the cross.

The simplest form is the Latin cross (*crux ordinaria*) which was from very early times also called God's Mark. Not only do we find the cross used as an emblem in church architecture, in masonic signs, family signs and in heraldry; we also find its appearance in apothecaries symbols and among the many hundreds of trade marks which were in use in the middle ages.

Among horse brasses we find the simplest kind of Latin cross (80); and others with the centre removed (75) so that the cross appears in silhouette. The ends of the latter cross are slightly rounded and its design suggests the cross pomee which is a common heraldic charge. The cross potent (25) can be found within an encircling border patterned in the fashion of a Roman pavement. This charge is still in use today and may be seen worn on the gowns of the Brethren of Saint Cross, Winchester, who occupy the old houses founded by Bishop Henry de Blois, in the eleventh century. Another form of the cross is the carbuncle (27) already mentioned.

Some people will be surprised to find an anchor on a horse brass (52, 98, 101) and at first sight this seems rather strange, but the ansated cross—the Egyptian symbol of life—is like a letter T with a small circle placed on top, and probably the Egyptian symbol was adapted and given a Christian purpose, ingeniously combining a pagan and a Christian idea.

An alternative explanation is that the anchor combines a cross and a crescent. In terms of Christian symbolism this represents the cross borne by Mary, who is symbolized by the crescent moon. The German artist Albrecht Durer—in his engravings to illustrate the Life of the Virgin (1511)—shows Mary and the Holy Child framed within a slender crescent.

Most crosses are symmetrical and this makes it easier to portray them within the normal shapes used for the horse brass.

Other emblems were used to decorate a cross brass, and one interesting specimen (80) shows a simple cross with thirteen holes punched in each of the spaces separating the arms. This is an unusual arrangement. Not only is thirteen traditionally an unlucky number, but it is repeated four times. The four spaces could of course represent the four seasons and the fifty two perforations each week of the year. Without its cross this brass would have significantly no meaning at all. We cannot say of course just how much appreciation the brass maker had of the designs he fashioned. They may simply have echoed patterns which had endured for so long that their individual meanings had been forgotten by those who made them.

GEOMETRICAL DESIGNS

The designs shown (1, 4, 16, 65, 85) are mostly based upon the circle. There is probably a very basic practical reason for this. Objects which were made to swing on the harness would perhaps cause less wear if they were rounded and without sharp or pointed edges. Among these designs, only a small selection of the variety available, we can see how the craftsman has with his compass constructed an intricate pattern of interwoven lines. Sometimes a brass is very light in the hand. Such brasses emphasise lines rather than mass. Both can be equally attractive, and there may well have been an alternative motive in designing a brass which contained a relatively small amount of metal. A brass of this kind would produce a slightly higher pitched jingle when it was mounted with its fellows, besides costing less to produce.

Among the geometrical brasses we could include those which display the signs so often used on playing cards. This may also explain why the heart shape appears so frequently. The rarest suit to find is the diamond, but perhaps fewer diamonds were made because their angular qualities produced uneven wear on the harness. The playing card brasses (4, 5, 17-19, 206) show the reader the considerable variations which these designs allow. Diamonds may be enclosed in circles or they may be shown as single emblems. They can also appear in rectangular shapes. They are sometimes shown as solid diamonds and occasionally the centre is cut away. The emblems may appear singly or they can be grouped. Again we can see how ingenious the designer craftsman was in the way these very simple emblems were arranged.

THE HORSE

One of the most obvious designs for a horse brass is the horse shoe. There are many variations. Those shown are fairly typical of the kind the collector may perhaps hope to acquire. Sometimes a left footed shoe is used and sometimes a right footed one (143, 144). Occasionally the horse shoe itself is enclosed within a design which is rather flamboyant (145). More often the horse shoe forms the framework for a design. The examples shown (128, 130, 135, 144-5) illustrate the variety of objects which can be found. The specimen (143) with three horse shoes enclosed in a larger one making a total of four is a very satisfactory symmetrical arrangement. If the reader studies the illustration carefully he will notice however that the horse shoes are intended for the same foot. The arrangement of nails is significant. Curiously most horse shoes on brasses hang downwards instead of in the traditionally 'lucky' upright position.

Sometimes the horse's head alone will appear framed by a horse shoe, and the two examples (128, 130) are very similar. The difference is in their details and these are important. One horse is shown with blinkers and the rest of the appropriate harness and the second wears no harness at all. The horses in (150, 156) wear collars and harness. In some ways this is a more satisfactory design. The similarity between these two horses will be noticed. It is not at all unusual to find virtually the same design, on a slightly smaller scale, employed within a border which has many different variations. One of the most pleasing designs we get among horse brasses are the ones which show a horse standing at rest (129, 146, 147). Usually horses, and other animals, look towards the left. One example (147) faces in the opposite direction. When we meet the collection of heraldic animals described below, we shall find that they too normally face towards the left.

Some of the horses appear to be standing on a thin straight line (132, 135, 141, 158, 178, 180). These are undoubtedly taken from a heraldic crest and although they may appear to be similar when seen on a horse brass they could in fact have come from a number of different sources. Some horses are at rest, others are walking and some are rampant—rearing up on their hind legs.

Two brasses have an undoubted racing flavour and one suspects that they are not very old. The galloping horse (162) is without a jockey but one is shown on another brass (137). The appearance of human figures on brasses is, in fact, unusual.

There is an endless variety of borders (140-145, 157-162, 175-180).

HARVEST

As far as the countryman is concerned the most important time of the year is the harvest, and many brasses use the symbols of the sheaf and the acorn. The brasses illustrated (34, 38, 39, 41, 209) will give us some idea of the sort of design we may expect to find. The wheatsheaf appears in several examples, sometimes encircled by a crescent (33, 38).

Most of the harvest brasses seem to be contained in a circular design which may allude to the endless rotation of the seasons. Designs which are the least pleasing are the flat plates with an intaglio impression of a wheatsheaf; these are probably relatively late additions to the horse brass world.

Another notable characteristic of the harvest brass is the designers' inclination to surround the wheatsheaf with a multitude of pierced circles (34). Heraldry has its share of wheatsheafs and the Peverel badge provides but one example of its use. The wheatsheaf has always been a popular inn sign.

Great skill is shown in the way some brasses display an arrangement of acorns interspersed with oak leaves (32). The use of the oak leaf and its seed (32, 35, 41, 209) is interesting. Acorns appear erect (41) or pendant and there does not seem to be any particular significance attached to either, but acorns and oak trees have another significance. Many an inn sign proclaims the fact that our forefathers at least had not forgotten the time when King Charles II eluded his pursuers by hiding in the luxuriant foliage of a stout English oak.

From a more patriotic age various customs are recorded on "Oak Apple Day"—29th May—which was the birthday of Charles II and the day of his public entry into London after the Restoration. Even towards the end of Victoria's reign an oak bough was fixed to the church flagstaff at Edlesborough, Bucks, and a similar custom was observed in Cheshire. Royal Oak customs are still observed in Northampton, Warwick and Worcester. We can find enough evidence to allow that at least some horse brass designs may have been inspired by this. Dr. Halley provided another memorial to him by naming the constellation Robur Caroli in 1676.

BELLS

The use of noise is a universal method of frightening away evil spirits. Naturally enough the jingle of the harness helped in this way but some brasses set out quite deliberately to create noise. In terms of twentieth century decibels of course heir "noise" is a mere tinkle. It is nevertheless pleasant and the examples shown (28-31, 103, 125) give us once again some impression of the variety of brasses with bells. There are single, twin and triple bells. Three of the specimens contain their bells in a flat plate which is cut out for the purpose. The odd specimen (29) employs the crescent and a bell suspended within its encircling arms and gives us perhaps one of the simplest and most beautiful of the many hundreds of designs. These tiny bells are themselves works of art—measuring no more than an inch across. Most of them, like the brasses, were cast, painstakingly polished and fitted with minute clappers.

It is still possible from time to time for the collector to find an odd bell which has become detached from its original brass. These bells themselves are worth collecting even if they have lost their brasses. You may come across one in a junk shop or even dig one up in the garden.

Bell brasses combine two methods of protection—they reflect the evil eye and scare it with their noise. They must represent the earliest kind of comprehensive insurance against catastrophe! We know that simple bells made from riveted plates were used by the Celts in the Dark Ages. Bells from this period are usually made of iron and examples have been found where the iron has been covered with a thin layer of bronze. Cast bells of great age are not so frequently found but a few parish churches possess small bells—often called sanctus bells because they were sounded during the elevation of the Host—which date from the fourteenth century. The practice of attaching bells to animals—especially sheep, oxen and horses—could easily date from such a distant past and some sheep bells, which were still in use in Sussex until the late 1930's, were fashioned from iron plates riveted together.

R. Thurston Hopkins—writing in *The Lure of Sussex*, C. Palmer (1928)—gives an account of sheep bells. There were three kinds of bells in use in those days which he calls the "canister" bell (with a wide mouth), the "clucket" bell (which had a crown slightly wider than the mouth) and the "rumbler" (a spherical shaped bell enclosing a metal ball that rolled about at the slightest movement). He observes that these rumblers, although used for some horses, are not attached to wagon-horses. The spherical bells (or crotals to give them another name) were made in assorted sizes, and they were used by cows, hansom-cab horses, and fire engine horses as well as by sheep. Those used in Sussex were made at Aldbourne, Wilts., by Robert Wells. His foundry was later absorbed by the famous Mears and Stainbank of Whitechapel Road, London.

It seems as if the tradition began to fade at about this time. A mere eight years later Thomas Hennel—in *Change in the Farm,* Cambridge University Press (1936)—was able to say that the use of horse brasses was in decline. They were still being cast at Wolverhampton in those days of course, and it seems likely that many later brasses never in fact felt the slap of the martingale before they found their way into the curio market. The cautious collector will always look for the signs of wear mentioned in a later chapter.

The use of the spherical crotal bell on horses is confirmed by Albrecht Durer. His engraving of a Great Triumphal Car (1515) contains some fascinating details of the horses used to move its massive weight. Their rich trappings are festooned with crotal bells—large and small. Each horse's neck is ringed with a garland of bells, and on the bit and headband we can see an embroidered rosette bearing a sun-wheel. The straps along the flanks repeat the sun-wheel motifs, and for good measure we also see a radiant sun with eyes to return any evil gaze.

INANIMATE OBJECTS

So far a good deal has been said about the countryman's use of the horse brass. We must not overlook the fact that thousands of horses worked only in the town. The coalman's cart, the brewer's dray and the miller's wagon have only recently disappeared.

Brasses used by people following specific callings naturally tended to include symbols associated with their work. The barrel (122, 123) appeared as a decoration for the brewery horse and it was used along with brasses bearing much older emblems. Sacks (124, 127) suggest the coalman or the corn merchant and the specimens illustrated could be appropriate for both. Less easy to define is the bell (125) which may have come from a bell founder's horse, or it may perhaps have been intended just as a symbol of noise.

The significance of the anchor (52, 98, 101) was discussed earlier, but another origin might have been the ship's chandler who found it a suitable device. It may possibly have shared a martingale with the ship (126) in full sail. This latter brass is otherwise a difficult design to explain.

A few horse drawn railway carts were in use until the 1950's and their horses too would have worn brasses. The railway brasses (54, 55) bear an almost identical locomotive with a single large driving wheel. This type of engine represents the very first kind that ran on English railways. Although the brasses themselves may not be more than eighty years old the design of the locomotive they show is certainly much older.

Every collector from time to time comes across specimens which are difficult to classify and which bear objects that are not always easy to identify. One specimen (53) shows a lyre. Why a musical instrument should have been worn by a horse is not immediately obvious. A specimen bearing a building (51) can provide many hours of thought and provoke a certain amount of research. This building is not easy to identify and without any exact knowledge of the brass's history one can only guess what it is intended to represent: perhaps the Tower of Babel.

HERALDIC CRESTS

Some of the adornments used to protect horses from evil influences were probably derived from the embellishments given to mediaeval war horses. The war horse, the property of the nobleman, helped to establish a connection between the nobility and the ploughman. We can find many examples of the nobleman's crest being used as a design for a horse brass. A crest is not part of a shield of arms but appears above it and is normally shown on a heraldic wreath of twisted ribbon. This was a band of material which was originally woven around the knight's helmet to support whatever figure or device he wished to carry.

The following examples give some indication of the type of animal which may be found used in this way. The lion, being the king of the beasts, will be found represented on many horse brasses. The lions shown (189, 198) are in two different positions. The first shows a lion walking from right to left. Its heraldic description is a lion passant. The other is standing on its hind legs and is described as rampant.

The lion has pride of place among heraldic beasts and this is no doubt partly due to the fact that it was adopted by the monarch in the early days of English heraldry. It has appeared since the reign of William I on the royal arms where it may still be seen today. A third lion was added to the two displayed by the Norman kings (from 1066 to 1154) and they have always been shown passant guardant (similar to 186). The lions on the two English quarters of the present Royal Arms should not be confused with the Scottish lion rampant which may be seen in the second quarter of the English royal shield—and on the shillings minted for use in Scotland.

The Royal Arms of England are supported by a lion and a unicorn. This latter mythical beast (50, 134, 136, 152, 178) is often found on horse brasses. The unicorn is one of the most elegant creatures used in heraldry, but it made its appearance long before heralds had blazoned their first shield. Unicorns appear frequently in the Old Testament.

Ancient tradition held that the only way to capture this fabulous beast was to leave a young virgin in one of the places to which it resorted. When the beast saw the maiden it would then lie quietly beside her, rest its head in her lap and fall asleep. Then the hunter could seize his unwary prey. The act of resting its head in a virgin's lap provided early Christians—so we are told—with a sufficient excuse to employ it as a Christian symbol. The creature's horn was highly prized in the mediaeval period as an antidote to all poison—it was therefore symbolic of the conquering of sin by the Messiah. Early printers favoured religious emblems and some adopted the unicorn as part of their device—John Harrison (1603) carried on his business at the "Unicorn and Bible" in Paternoster Row, London. The reputation of the healing powers of its horn led the Apothecaries' Company to adopt a unicorn as a supporter on its arms. A unicorn's horn was of more value than gold in the middle ages and the goldsmiths too found this a suitable emblem to hang outside their shops. An inventory of royal jewels (Queen Elizabeth I) shows "a piece of unicorn's horn" placed first—Pepys's Library ; Bib. Harl. 5953, vol. i, p. 403—which is an indication of its relative value. Many inns also bore the sign of the unicorn and we can be quite certain that it was a well known symbol. As far as horse brasses are concerned the creature provided an appropriate emblem for those who wished to protect a horse. No doubt a few unicorns found their way on to brasses via a nobleman's arms, but it seems almost equally probable that unicorn brasses could have much older origins.

Next to the lion the eagle probably ranks highest among heraldic creatures. The most usual position adopted by this regal bird on shields and crests is with its wings outstretched —or displayed, to use the precise heraldic terminology. Many different heraldic achievements could have inspired eagle designs (45, 195).

Another fabulous beast we find adorning heraldic shields is the griffin. This creature is half eagle and half lion. Two examples (49, 165) are shown. The first is a demi-griffin rampant, and the second is sejant—sitting—and supports a shield with its dexter fore-leg. We find griffins on various arms and crests including the Spencers'. Ancient seals show that the Earls of Devon and Derby used the griffin as a badge.

The swan (47, 193) is frequently found in English heraldry. One of the best known bearers of the swan badge was Thomas Woodstock—son of King Edward III—who displayed a swan argent (silver). Thomas de Warwick (d. 1242) also had a silver swan as a badge—a red coronet around its neck helped to distinguish it from the Woodstock badge. Each year the custom of swan upping is carried out along the river Thames and this may help to explain why there were once so many Swan inns along the banks of London's river. Trade tokens, issued by traders to combat the extreme shortage of small change in the seventeenth century, still exist showing a swan walking on Old London Bridge (1657). There were many sources then from which the swan brasses could derive. When we see a swan represented on a heraldic wreath however (47) we may guess at its noble origins.

Another bird popular with artists in the middle ages, and found on a good many brasses, is the pelican. The tradition is that it pierced its own breast to feed its young (170) and for this reason it became used as a Christian symbol. The "pelican in its piety" will be found on the Arms of Corpus Christi College, Oxford.

Both stags and deer have now retreated to the stately homes or national parks. Two hundred years or so ago things were rather different. It is no surprise to find stags appearing on horse brasses (169, 172, 196-7). They are symbols of a lost age when wild animals—especially those which belonged to the lord of the manor—were free to roam through anyone's corn. The stag, or its near relation, is found on many heraldic designs. They support the Buckinghamshire County Council arms and the families of Dalziel, Downshire and Gort also find a place for them. Like so many other symbols the stag has been credited with a religious significance. Its occurrence in the catacombs of Rome is claimed to be an allusion to Psalm 42—"Like as the hart desireth the water brook, so longeth my soul after thee, O God!". Whatever significance we may place upon the presence of the stag on the horse brass it does seem as if a considerable number of them owe their patterns to heraldry.

An unlikely animal to appear upon a horse brass is the elephant. One type of brass (187) has the name 'Alice' written around its edge, in honour of a well known inmate of the London Zoo. This circumstance alone can scarcely account for the considerable variety of elephants the collector may encounter (182, 187, 188). Heraldic sources obviously account for a number. An elephant appears as a supporter on the arms of the Earl of Caledon, another on the arms of the Earl of Powis. As supporters the creatures are in a rampant position but on a brass the elephant is normally shown standing. In the middle ages the elephant was nearly always portrayed bearing a castle upon its back. (The Chinese chess rook is still shown in this form.) An elephant was also used by the Cutlers' Company as a crest, as it provided the ivory used in the trade. The Elephant and Castle is of course a well known site in London and the name recalls the presence of a coaching inn which received its name as a result of an "elephant's" skeleton being uncovered there in the early part of the eighteenth century. A spear with a flint head was found close to it and this gave rise to the improbable legend that the animal was slain in a conflict between the Romans and the Britons. Horse brasses seem to ignore the castles but the elephant is well represented. Its use on the horse brass was almost certainly inspired by its use in heraldry.

During the middle ages and even into the modern era bear baiting was an accepted part of public entertainment. A number of inn signs no doubt owe their origin to this barbarous pastime. Horse brasses (174) may have borrowed their bears from heraldry, but bear baiting often took place in stable yards near horses' stalls and this proximity may be a connection.

More prosaic, but none the less interesting creatures may be found like the cat and the dog, which had a place (164, 23) in heraldry. Many heraldic bearings include the old English hunting dog—the talbot. In the distant past it was the usual practice to provide servants with uniforms bearing a suitable emblem which portrayed their responsibilities often in the form of a rebus. Thus it was that the butler's bore cups and the fletcher's a pheon (arrowhead). The grosvenors —grand huntsmen to the Dukes of Normandy—displayed as a crest the talbot (23) which ran before them in the royal chase.

Among the heraldic badges we find that Sir Bryan Stapylton used a talbot passant with an ear slit and bleeding. The Earls of Shrewsbury (family name Talbot) naturally made use of it as a badge usually in the form of a talbot passant argent (silver).

COMMEMORATIVE BRASSES

Towards the end of Victoria's long reign commemorative brasses began to make their appearance, particularly during Jubilee Year in 1887. Some of these jubilee brasses (115) were stamped out and this variety lacks the quality of the cast kind. A few (117, 120) have quite a crude appearance. Others were embellished with crowns (111, 112, 118, 119) that were rivetted to the flat plates. Most of the lettering on such brasses seems to have been stamped on ; and (118) the letters "AVE" reflect the light around their edges showing us that they were formed in this way.

The year 1897 marked the Diamond Jubilee and this brought forth a fresh crop of brasses (112). In a patriotic age it was natural to find slogans such as "Union is Strength", "The Victorian Record" and "Victoria the Good" added to the designs. The dates on the jubilee brasses 1887, 1897 and those made when Victoria died in 1901 can be misleading. Astute brass makers reproduced many of these designs when brasses became popular again in 1945 following the austerity of wartime Britain. More will be said below about reproductions, but it is sufficient here for the collector to note that dated brasses are not always as old as they appear.

Brasses bearing the head of King Edward VII, 1907, were made but by this time the art was in decline. King George V's accession produced appropriate brasses (118) which by now followed the accepted patterns of those made for earlier monarchs. The last royal brass was probably made in 1937. What was perhaps one of the last commemorative designs to appear shows the well known profile of Sir Winston Churchill with his cigar. From the design point of view any brass which attempts to portray a human face is not likely to be very successful, and, historic connections apart, these brasses do not rank among the best designs.

FLY TERRETS — "SWINGERS"

In place of the plumes (shown on page 17) many horses wore a fly-terret (or swinger) upon the crown. The usage depended upon local tradition. Another flyer—often with bells —was to be found on the saddle.

Swingers (199-210) were attached to the crown band, and they doubtless derived their name from the swinging amulets they encompassed. Most are circular in shape but exceptions (206) may be found. Like the brasses the designs employed on the swinger fall into the same main groups. A few had plain discs (202), but more were fashioned into a design of one type or another. Variations of the sun-wheel motif and of the crescent (210) are fairly common. Symbols from nature

—the thistle (208), the acorn (209) and the flower—are also used as are animals and playing card designs. Certain swingers—but not of outstanding quality—contain commemorative emblems but all these seem to date from this century.

The swinger with a bell is a rarity outside a museum, although from time to time the collector may be fortunate enough to find bells which have parted company with their original terret. Terrets complete with bells need to be scrutinised carefully before they are purchased. It is possible to pay a high price for one with odd bells unless these details are noticed. This is not to say that such a piece is without value or interest. The purist, however, will always wish to add the best pieces to his collection and it is a good thing to develop a critical eye before too many imperfect specimens are amassed. A terret with an odd bell of course need to be better than no terret at all. If the enthusiast has the opportunity to collect a few spare parts he may be able with luck to supply any deficiency with a later purchase. It is a good idea to carry a brief but accurate list of spares, with their main dimensions, with you because you can never tell when the opportunity to add a useful piece will occur. The size of a bell may be a helpful thing to look up before you decide upon your price for an imperfect terret and haggling with the dealer begins!

Terrets are not so easy to find and the opportunity to add one—especially a good example—is something that should not be missed. Some terrets are quite old—more than a century or so—and the prudent collector will always want to examine a prospective purchase carefully before he makes a bid. The obvious signs of age—like wear at the joints and the patination brought about with years of elbow grease—need to be studied before you can make a decision about the probable period of origin. Design features will give a clue, but they are a guide to age rather than a precise indicator. Sometimes a terret has a centre which replaces the original one. The replacement may differ in size sufficiently for it to be quite obvious (201?). A study of the rivet at the top may in such circumstances help you to decide about the marks left by possible re-riveting. With a little experience points of this kind become part of a collector's instinct.

Another feature which may help to determine the presence of a replacement is the relative colour of the terret and the swinger. If they came from the same brass they will be alike, but a good many terrets probably started off with swingers that did not match exactly. Anything that is a subject for the collectors' attention will produce a few fakes of one sort or another—and personal experience is probably the best mentor for a collector to heed. Books can suggest ways of looking but they will never account for all the subtle points of texture, colour and weight that go to make up the established collector's knowledge.

CARE AND CLEANING

Removing lacquer

If an old piece of brass has been lacquered, the lacquer is sometimes chipped and the exposed parts tarnish, giving it a piebald appearance which will ruin the look of the piece.

Removing lacquer is not the easiest task, but it is a worthwhile one. Acetone may be used to remove old cellulose, the most common lacquer on older pieces, but the new synthetics such as polyurethane or acrylates are particularly stubborn.

Routine cleaning and care

Polishes containing a tarnish prevention do exist for both brass and copper but they are not too effective. There are various technical reasons for this, although research is continuing to find a compound which will attach itself more firmly to the copper and brass surface.

Brass is a harder metal than copper. Its yellow colour is characteristic, but if treated with very acid materials it can become an unpleasant 'red' shade. There are three metal polish formulae on the market which clean brass. These are liquid polishes, such as Brasso, paste polishes and impregnated non-scratch wadding. Any one of these three can be used effectively. As with silver and copper, brass can be stained or soiled by reacting with oxygen and sulphur, which are present in air as well as the constituents of foodstuffs, etc. Being a relatively soft metal it will scratch and abrade fairly readily.

The polishing of horse brasses, which are heavily patterned or chased articles, is best done with a soft brush and then rubbed up with a soft duster. Avoid scratching the metal with fingernails by wearing gloves. Rubber gloves can be worn for putting on the polish, while cotton gloves, worn for the polishing will ensure that no fingerprints are left on metal. Dusters used specifically for polishing very old items should be kept in polythene bags away from grit and dirt. Certain polishes already have in-built sponges and applicators, which are handy.

Cleaning and restoring badly marked or verdigris covered brass

If the brass is just heavily tarnished it should be cleaned with a conventional polish.

If the brass has for some reason been burnt it can be cleaned with a cut lemon dipped in a mild paste abrasive or in salt.

Verdigris should *never* be treated with anything containing hydrochloric acid, since this will ruin the surface. If the verdigris is very thick, and the piece old and of some value, rather than spoil a good design or marking, take the piece to a reputable ironmonger, where there will normally be an expert on restoring metals. Most verdigris, however, can be removed with a mixture of vinegar and coarse kitchen salt. Then a dip in hot soapy water will prepare the brass for regular polishing with a metal polish.

It is the abrasive action of the polish which removes tarnish and the polishing action which causes the healing or 'flowing' of the surface metal into the scratches to cover the gaps. Therefore, an old piece which has not been polished for some time will need constant care and polishing in order to 'smooth' the surface and heal scratches.

INDEX

Titles in the Discovering series
(with their series numbers)

*From your bookseller or from Shire Publications Ltd.,
Cromwell House, Church Street, Princes Risborough,
Aylesbury, Bucks., U.K.*